TAIPANS

DOUG WECHSLER

ACADEMY OF NATURAL SCIENCES

The Rosen Publishing Group's
PowerKids Press™
New York

For all the slithering, creeping, and crawling beasts that have made my life so much richer.

About the Author
Wildlife biologist, ornithologist, and photographer Doug Wechsler has studied birds, snakes, frogs, and other wildlife around the world. Doug Wechsler works at The Academy of Natural Sciences of Philadelphia, a natural history museum. As part of his job, he travels to rain forests and remote parts of the world to take pictures of birds. He has taken part in expeditions to Ecuador, the Philippines, Borneo, Cuba, Cameroon, and many other countries.

Published in 2001 by The Rosen Publishing Group, Inc.
29 East 21st Street, New York, NY 10010

First Edition

Book Design: Michael de Guzman

Photo Credits: pp. 4, 8, 11 Bruce Coleman, Inc.; p. 7 © M. Harvey/DRK Photo; p. 12 © Stanley Breeden/DRK Photo; p. 15 © Frank Lane Picture Agency/CORBIS; p. 16 © Austin J. Stevens/Animals Animals; pp. 19, 22 © Fritz Prenzel/Animals Animals; p. 20 © George McCarthy/CORBIS.

Wechsler, Doug.
    Taipans / Doug Wechsler.
       p. cm.— (The really wild life of snakes)
    Includes index.
    Summary: This book describes the physical characteristics, behavior, and habitats of taipans, some of the most poisonous snakes in the world.
    ISBN 0-8239-5602-4
    1. Oxyuranus—Juvenile literature. 2. Poisonous snakes—Juvenile literature. [1. Snakes.] I. Title. II. Series.
    2000
S97.96—dc21

Manufactured in the United States of America

CONTENTS

LONG, FAST, AND DEADLY

They are long. They are fast. They are deadly. Some people say taipans are among the most dangerous snakes in the world. We will see about that! Taipans are fast-moving snakes with good eyesight. They are most active in the daytime. There are two **species** of taipans. They live in Australia and on the nearby island of New Guinea. Taipans are the longest **venomous** snakes in Australia. There are only a few venomous snakes from other parts of the world that are longer, such as the king cobra and the black mamba.

Taipans are some of the most poisonous snakes in the world. Luckily, many of them live in areas where there are not a lot of people.

Coastal taipans live near the coast of north and northeast Australia. They are one of the world's longest poisonous snakes. Coastal taipans can grow to 11 feet (3.4 m), but 8 feet (2.4 m) is more usual. They live in woodlands, in sugarcane fields, and on farms. Over the past 100 years, taipans have become more common as sugarcane farming has increased. The coastal taipan is usually a shy snake, but it is very dangerous if cornered. When it gets angry, it strikes quickly over and over again. The taipans of New Guinea are very similar to the coastal taipans.

Taipans live only in Australia and New Guinea. Australia and New Guinea were connected during the Ice Age so they have many species in common.

DOUG SAYS

THE NAME TAIPAN COMES FROM THE ABORIGINES, THE NATIVE PEOPLE OF AUSTRALIA. IT IS THE NAME FOR THE COASTAL TAIPAN.

INLAND TAIPANS

The inland taipan is also called "fierce snake." It lives only in the deserts of central Australia. When the sun is too hot, an inland taipan likes to hide deep in the cracks of the dry desert soil. Few people live in the deserts, so the inland taipan rarely gets a chance to bite anyone. An inland taipan usually grows to five feet (1.5 m). Even though it is famous for its strong **venom**, this snake is not usually as fierce as its name suggests. An inland taipan is not likely to bite people unless they disturb it. There are no records of anyone dying from the bite of this dangerous snake. Still, it is best to keep your distance.

The inland taipan is shorter and more poisonous than its cousin, the coastal taipan.

9

MY TWO FRONT TEETH

When taipans bite, venom shoots through the two long teeth in the front of the mouth. These two hollow teeth are called **fangs**. When a taipan's mouth is closed, the fangs do not fold back like the fangs of a viper or rattlesnake. Instead the fangs are fixed in place in the upper jaw. The fangs can grow to be one-half inch long (12.7 mm). The fangs are connected to the venom **sacs** by a tube. The sacs are located in the cheeks, where the deadly venom is stored. When a coastal taipan bites its **prey**, it does not hold on to its victim. It lets the prey go and then follows the scent trail to where the prey dies. The inland taipan, though, holds on to its meal until its prey dies.

Like other poisonous snakes, taipans have curved fangs. When the taipan closes its mouth, the fangs do not fold back like the long fangs of a rattlesnake.

DOUG SAYS

TAIPANS CAN BITE THROUGH THICK CLOTHING. IF THEIR FANGS BREAK, NEW FANGS WILL SOON TAKE THEIR PLACE.

DOUG SAYS

WRITERS LIKE TO DESCRIBE THE HEAD OF A TAIPAN AS "COFFIN SHAPED." THIS MAKES THEM SEEM EVEN MORE DANGEROUS THAN THEY ARE.

NOT THE DEADLIEST LAND SNAKE

Though taipans are dangerous, the danger has been **exaggerated**. It is true that drop for drop the venom of the inland taipan can kill more mice than any other land snake. (Scientists test the strength of snakes' venom on mice, not people.) Few people see inland taipans in the wild because the snakes live in the desert. Taipans are shy snakes. They would rather flee than bite. Most people are bitten when they try to catch or kill the snake. If a taipan is cornered, it strikes very fast. Coastal taipans kill about one person every year in Australia.

Compare that to Russell's vipers. Russell's vipers kill about 50,000 people each year in Asia.

A taipan will not attack a person unless the snake feels threatened.

TAIPAN RELATIVES

Taipans belong to a family of snakes called **elapids**. Most of Australia's land snakes are elapids. All elapids have very strong venom, although some, such as the bandy-bandy, never use it on people. Cobras, coral snakes, and black mambas are taipan relatives that live on other continents. All of these snakes have fixed fangs that do not move as the snakes bite their prey. They also have very strong venom and bad **reputations**. Their venom usually works on the **nervous systems** of their victims.

Cobras are relatives of taipans. Cobras can be found in Asia and Africa. This cobra uses its hood to make it look bigger. The hood also warns enemies that the snake is dangerous.

DOUG SAYS

ANTIVENOM MUST BE FRESH. NEW VENOM IS COLLECTED REGULARLY FROM LIVE TAIPANS. SOMEONE MUST HOLD THE SNAKE'S HEAD WHILE IT BITES INTO A THIN RUBBER SHEET OVER A BOTTLE. THIS METHOD OF COLLECTING THE VENOM IS USUALLY CALLED MILKING.

VENOM AND ANTIVENOM

The venom of both species of taipans, coastal and inland, is very strong. The venom is a mixture of nasty **chemicals**. The venom from one inland taipan bite is strong enough to kill 50,000 mice. The same amount of venom from a coastal taipan could kill 12,000 mice. Without medical treatment, most people bitten by taipans will die.

Doctors treat snakebites with **antivenom**. Antivenom is made by injecting small amounts of venom into a horse. The small amount of venom does not harm the horse. The horse's body makes chemicals to destroy the venom. The chemicals are separated from the horse's blood and made into antivenom.

This black mamba is about to be milked for its venom. The person handling the snake is an expert. People who study and handle snakes are called herpetologists.

EGGS AND YOUNG TAIPANS

In early summer, female taipans lay between 7 and 20 eggs. The eggs have leathery shells. It takes 10 to 14 weeks for the eggs to hatch. When the babies hatch they are about one foot (30 cm) long. Once they hatch, the babies are on their own. They must find their own food and shelter. They also must defend themselves, but they are well armed with fangs and venom.

Young males take at least a year and a half to become adults. Females start to lay eggs when they are at least two years old and about 3 1/2 feet (1.1 m) long. Taipans can live for 20 years or more.

Taipans take at least a year and a half to become adults. Female snakes have to be more than two years old to lay eggs.

DOUG SAYS
A MALE TAIPAN FINDS A FEMALE BY FOLLOWING HER SCENT TRAIL. THE MALE SMELLS THE TRAIL WITH HIS TONGUE.

WHAT TAIPANS DO FOR US

Taipans help people in a few ways. They eat lots of mice and rats. Taipans help to keep the numbers of these pests in check.

Scientists are studying taipan venom. They have learned about the different chemicals in the venom and what they do. At least one of the chemicals is used for medical testing. It can be used in a test to see if a person has a disease called **lupus**. Perhaps one day taipans will save more people than they kill.

Rats and other rodents are a favorite food of taipans. A taipan's venom kills these small animals very quickly.

TIPTOEING TAIPANS

Taipans are fast-moving snakes. You could probably outrun a taipan in the open, but not in tall grass. The tall grass would slow you down, but not the taipan. How do taipans and other snakes move? When a snake moves, it looks like a big "S" or like more than one "S." A snake pushes the underside of each curve in its body against rocks, sticks, or bumps in the ground. As it pushes, a taipan moves forward, following the same "S" path. Wherever the head moves, the body follows. Taipans move quietly, as if they were tiptoeing. Sometimes a taipan travels with its head and neck raised off the ground. It gets a better view this way.

GLOSSARY

antivenom (AN-ty-ven-um) A medicine used to treat snakebites.

chemicals (KEH-mih-kuls) Substances that can be mixed with other substances to cause reactions.

elapids (EH-leh-peds) A family of venomous snakes with fangs.

exaggerated (ig-ZAH-jeh-rayt-ed) To say something is bigger than it really is.

fangs (FANGZ) Hollow teeth that inject venom.

lupus (LOO-pes) A type of disease that affects the skin and other tissues.

nervous systems (NER-ves SIS-tems) Systems of nerve fibers, nerve cells, and other nerve tissue in people or animals. In a person, the nervous system includes the brain and spinal cord and controls all body activities.

prey (PRAY) An animal that is eaten by another animal for food.

reputations (reh-pyoo-TAY-shunz) What things people think and say about a person, animal, or object.

sacs (SAKS) Pouchlike parts in a plant or animal.

species (SPEE-sheez) A single kind of plant or animal. For example, all people are one species.

venom (VEN-um) A poison passed by one animal into another through a bite or sting.

venomous (VEN-um-us) Having a poisonous bite.

INDEX

WEB SITES

To learn more about taipans, check out these Web sites:

http://www.kingsnake.com/aho/taipans.html
http://www.rochedalss.qld.edu.au/taipan.htm
http://www.pharmacology.unimelb.edu.au/PHARMWWW/avruweb/
    Taipans.htm